ADULT COLORING BOOK TO RELIEVE STRESS AND ANXIETY · A YEAR-LONG

365

DAYS OF
MANDALAS

THIS COLORING BOOK BELONGS TO:

_____

HAPPY COLORING!

Book and cover design by David Miles

Mandalas illustrated by the following talented Shutterstock.com artists:
Pure Sight lab, ViSnezh, Kseniya Parkhimchyk, An Vino, and Katika.

Additional cover elements licensed as follows: colored pencils (PixDeluxe/
Shutterstock.com); colored background (shekaka/Shutterstock.com);
cover mandala design (irmairma/Shutterstock.com); spine border
(Bariskina/Shutterstock.com).

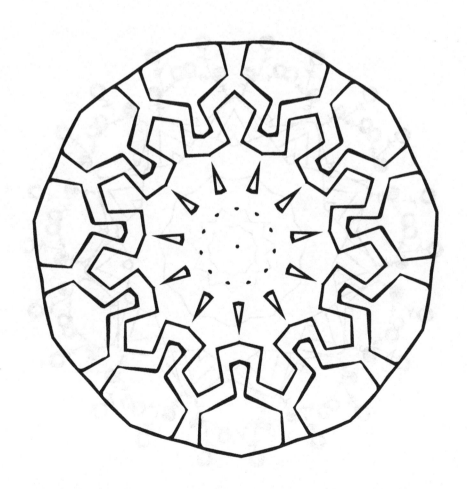

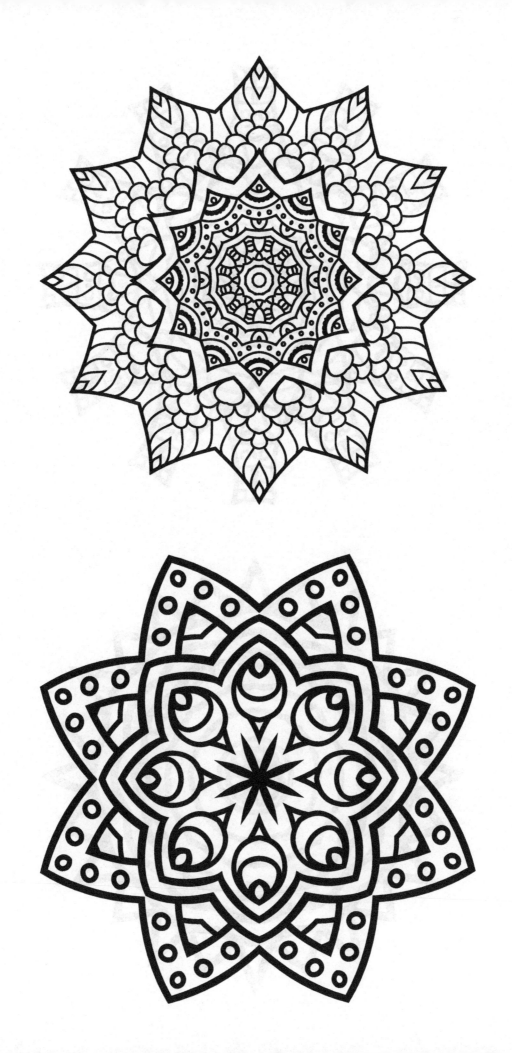

Made in the USA
Monee, IL
27 July 2024

62635996R10142